Contents

Tudor Maps	2
Churches	6
Monasteries	10
Homes	12
Schools and Colleges	16
Inns and Pubs	18
Mayors	20
Documents	22
Objects	24

St Marie's
Catholic Junior School
Merttens Drive
Rugby
CV22 7AF
Tel/Fax 01788 543636
E-mail: admin3562@we-learn.com

Tudor Maps

Have you ever thought about investigating what your town or village was like in Tudor times? You could start by looking at a copy of an old map, which was drawn around four hundred years ago.

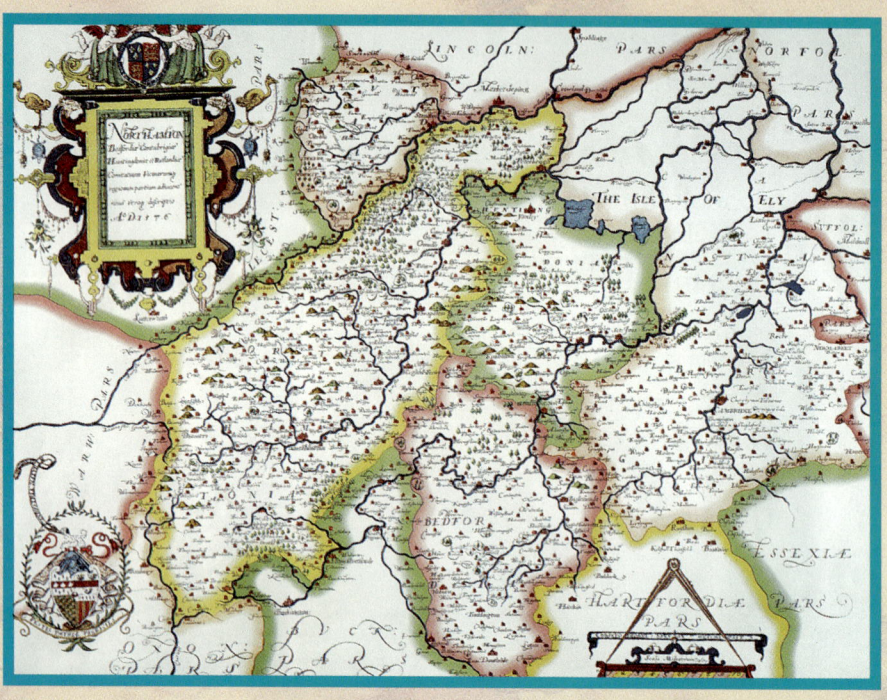

Christopher Saxton drew this map in 1576, when he travelled all over England and Wales drawing maps for an atlas.

We can see what the countryside was like and the names of the villages. Can you see the pictures which show woods, hills, marshes and heathland?

There are rivers on the map, but no big roads. In Tudor times it was easier to get about by boat than by cart on the bumpy roads.

 Maps of your town or village:

Ask at your local library for copies of Tudor maps. John Speed and William Norden were two other famous Tudor map makers.

There were also many maps of towns drawn in Tudor times. They show us where the streets, churches, houses and bridges stood. Many streets still have the same names today.

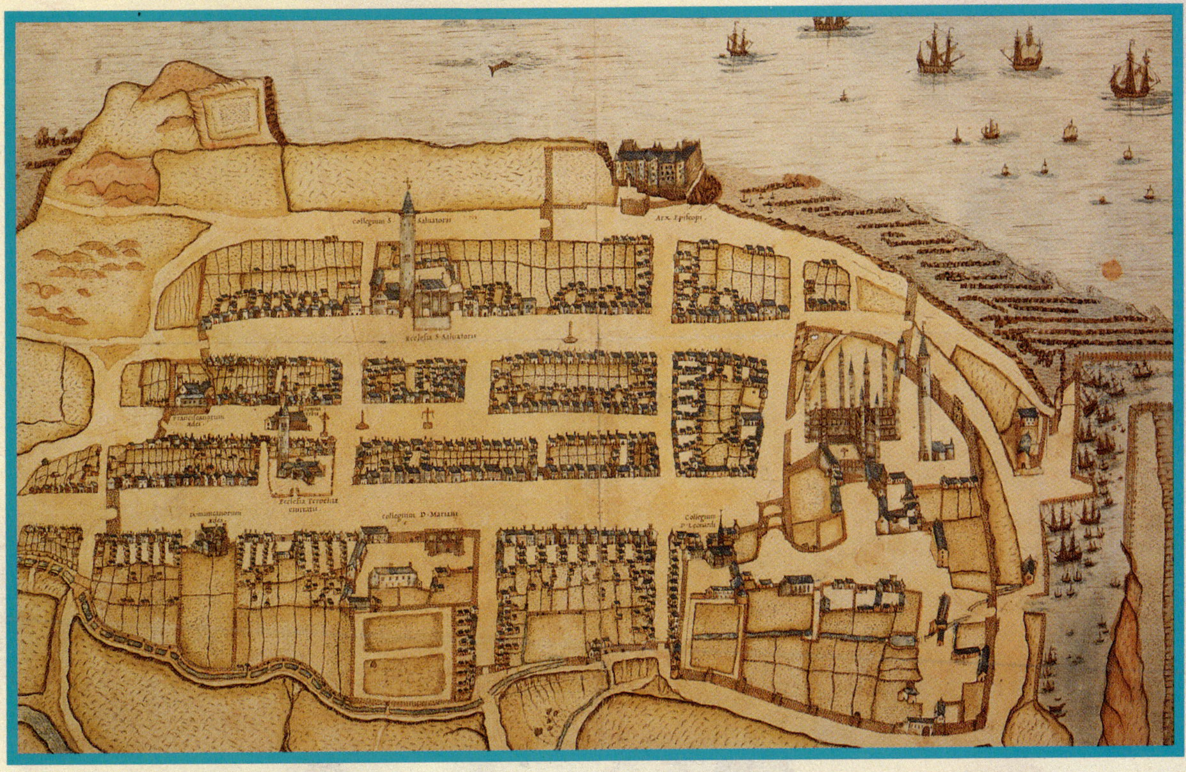

This map of St Andrews in Scotland was drawn in 1550. Find:

- the wall round the town.
- the ships in the harbour.
- the castle on a rock above the sea.
- the cathedral.

If you visit St Andrews today you will find some of the buildings still there, in the places shown on the map.

 More clues to look for:

The rivers, harbours, bridges, castles and churches that were drawn on the maps. Street names that are still the same as on the Tudor maps.

Some of the first Tudor writers to study geography described what they saw instead of drawing maps.

This monument to John Stow shows him writing his great book called *The Survey of London*.

Here is what he wrote about a small hill beside the Tower of London:

Upon this hill is always readily prepared ... a large scaffold and gallows of timber, for the execution of such traitors ... as are delivered out of the Tower ... there to be executed.

A modern clue to the place John Stow wrote about.

London Underground sign

John Leland travelled on horseback all over England and Wales. He wrote down what he saw in small villages as well as in towns and ports.

This is what he wrote about Birmingham:

It is a good market town ... and as far as I could see it has only one parish church. In the town are many smiths who make knives and all kinds of cutting tools for a living.

View of Birmingham, 1656

The church John Leland saw is called St Martin's church and is still standing today. The rest of Birmingham was rebuilt in Victorian times

 Other Tudor travellers:

William Camden and William Harrison were two other Tudor travellers who wrote about the places they visited.

5

Churches

Most old churches and cathedrals were built long before Tudor times. However, some church buildings were changed and improved in the fifteenth and sixteenth centuries. To find out about the Tudors, look for the parts of the church they built.

It was the fashion then to build in a style that people call the **perpendicular** style.

Kings College Chapel, Cambridge

 Church building clues to look for:

Look out for pointed stone arches and tall decorated window frames.
Use the church guide book to help you to find out which parts were built in Tudor times.

Tudor stone masons built this ceiling in the perpendicular style. It is called fan vaulting. Can you see why?

Perpendicular

A style of building using delicate stonework, tall columns and high windows.

Tudor builders were also good at carving wood.

Wooden beams were used to hold up some church roofs. Woodworkers carved patterns where the beams joined.

Southwark Cathedral, London

Altarnun Church, Cornwall

This carving was done for the end of a church bench.

We know it was done in Tudor times because of the clothes worn by the musician. He is playing a viol, an instrument like a violin.

 More woodwork clues to look for:

Wood panels that look like folded linen (see page 12), carved wood screens, large pulpits.

7

We can find out about people's lives from the graves inside churches and other memorials from Tudor times.

This is a rubbing of a brass in a church in Oxfordshire. It was made in memory of Joan Bradshawe, her two husbands, who both died before her, and her eight children. We can find out quite a lot about the family from the picture on the brass and the inscription underneath it.

 Brasses:
These were put on the walls or floors of churches. Brass plates were made from a mixture of copper, zinc, tin and lead.

Some rich Tudor families gave money to the church when they were alive to pay for their grave when they died. Many of them also paid for a sculptor to make a statue of them in stone.

This is called a table tomb. It is the grave of Thomas and Alice Gamul, who lived in Chester. Their stone statues give us a lot of information about Tudor clothes.

 More information to look for:

Some graves tell us how old the people were when they died, what job they did, where they lived, what they wore and how many children they had.

Monasteries

In the time of King Henry VII, the first Tudor monarch, there were monasteries and nunneries everywhere. There was probably at least one near to where you live.

Nuns like these lived in a nunnery. As well as praying in church, they ran farms, schools and hospitals.

King Henry VIII ordered all the monasteries to be closed.

Today the only clues about where the monks or nuns lived may be in your street names.

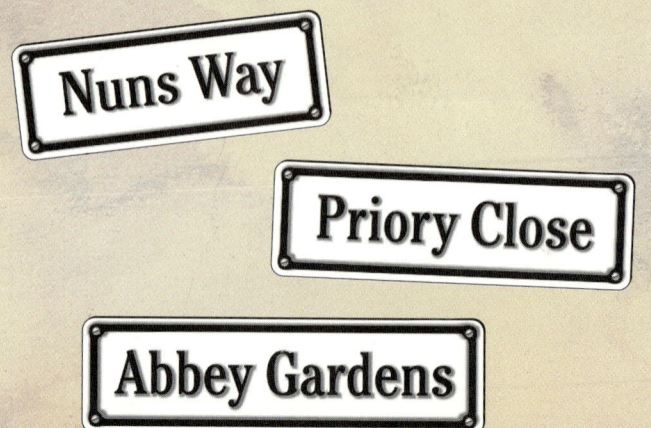

In a few places, the ruins of some of the old monastic buildings have survived until today.

Castle Acre Priory, Norfolk

This ruin was once the church in the old monastery. If you walk round the site you can also find the monks' dining room, kitchen and the cells where they slept.

King Henry gave or sold the land which used to belong to the monastery to his friends.

They used it, and even some of the building stone, to build grand houses for themselves.

More monastery clues:

Look in big cathedrals for cloisters where the monks walked.

Names of houses, schools, colleges, and gardens.

Homes

The Tudors built homes in many different materials and in different styles.

The largest homes tell us about the very rich who could afford stone, brick and glass.

When this house was built a visitor said that there was "more glass than wall". The glass was made by hand and was very expensive. It was made in small panes which were fitted together with lead.

Hardwick Hall, Derbyshire

Inside, many of the rooms were panelled in wood that looked like folded linen.

 Tudor houses to look for:

Find out if there is a large Tudor house you can visit. Many of them now belong to the National Trust or to English Heritage.

Merchants, who made their money from buying and selling, had money to spend on their homes too.

Paycocke's House, Essex

Thomas Paycocke, a woollen merchant, built this house. It had a warehouse and office as well as rooms for his family.

Find:
- the wooden framework. Houses like this are called 'timber-framed'.
- the bricks between the wood. Only people who had money could afford to pay for bricks.
- the brick chimney.
- the carving along the front of the house. Thomas Paycocke had to pay for this too.

Yeomen farmers owned land in Tudor times. They built their houses with strong materials. You will find many of them that are still lived in today in country villages.

Yeoman's house, Montgomeryshire

This house was built with a timber frame. Local stone was often used to fill in the spaces in between the wood. It was cheaper than hand-made bricks. Where do you think the material for the roof came from?

Many yeomen families also had furniture made from oak.

Farm workers did not own land and were the poorest people in Tudor times. They were called 'cottagers' and they built themselves small homes with whatever materials they could find in the countryside. Some cottages had wooden beams. Others were made from peat or mud mixed with twigs and animal hair or straw. Only a few farmworkers' homes have survived.

 More village clues:
Timber-framed farmhouses and barns.
Common land, woods and ponds that were there in Tudor times.
Village stocks.

Schools and Colleges

When the monasteries were sold, the schools run by the monks and nuns had to close.

King Henry VIII, his son King Edward VI and other wealthy people gave money to build some new schools called 'grammar' schools. Only boys went to grammar schools and they had to pay fees to go there. Many of them were the sons of merchants and yeomen.

This school in Chelmsford still has the name of the founder, King Edward VI, but the building has been changed many times since then.

Some boys who could not pay fees went to charity schools. They were given their school clothes as well as books and lessons.

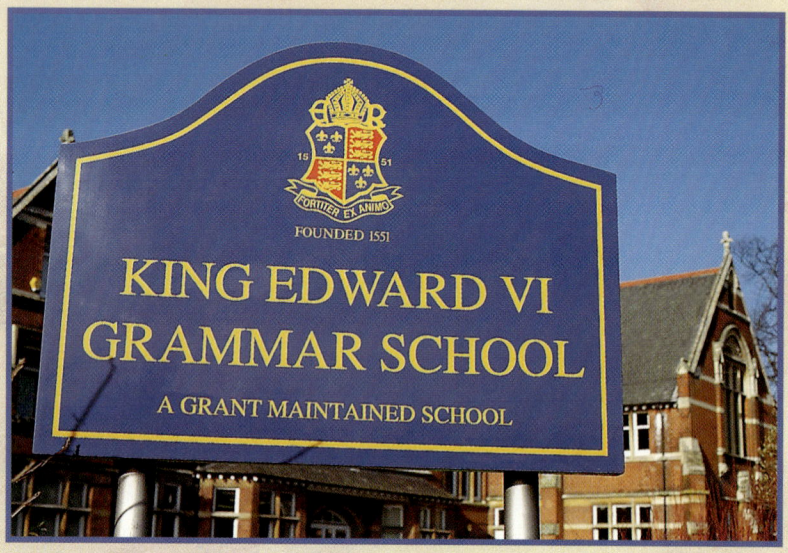

Some of the schools are still open today. The boys and girls wear Tudor clothes as their school uniform. The schools are sometimes called 'bluecoat' schools. Can you see why?

 School clues:

When was the first school in your town opened? Look for signs of 'charity' school children.

There was a grammar school in every large town, but only a few universities. Boys could go to a university when they were fifteen years old and new colleges were opened in Tudor times at Oxford, Cambridge, Glasgow, St Andrews and Aberdeen. Some of the new colleges replaced monasteries.

Lady Margaret Beaufort, a close friend of the Royal family, paid for this college building.

Christ's College, Cambridge

Find:

- her coat of arms. This shows that she was from a noble family.
- the Tudor Rose with the crown above. This shows it was built in Tudor times.
- the gate called a portcullis with the crown above. This is the badge of the House of Commons today.

Inns and Pubs

Many old village pubs have stood in the same place for over a thousand years. Pub signs are useful clues about how old the pubs are.

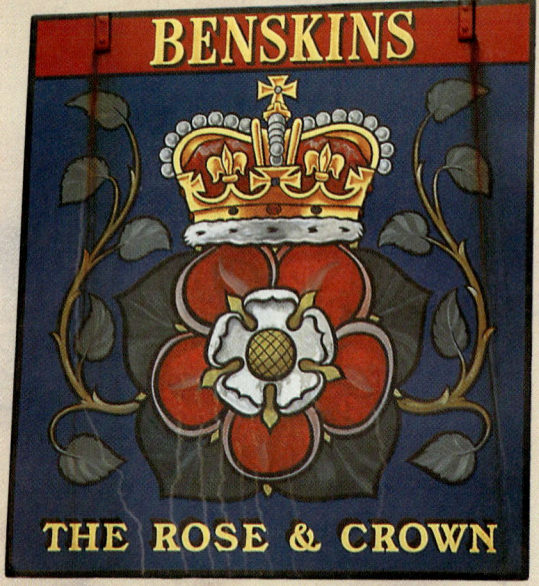

The Rose in this pub sign is a Tudor rose, the badge of the Tudor kings and queens. The name Rose and Crown was probably given to the pub in honour of the Tudor monarchs.

Always look carefully at the wood timbers on old pubs. Do they look like trunks of real trees? If so, the building is probably Tudor.

Modern builders sometimes put thin wooden planks on a building to make it look old. Usually the buildings are not old enough to be Tudor.

 Pub names:

Collect a list of pub names. Sort them out into the names you think are modern, Victorian, Tudor and earlier than Tudor.

Every town had an inn in Tudor times. Travellers found a meal, a bed for the night and a stable for their horse. Sometimes they were entertained by groups of musicians or actors who also stayed at the inn.

Today some of the old inns are still used as hotels.

George Inn, Southwark

 Clues to look for:

Is there a hotel with an inn yard near to where you live? How old do you think the building is?

People can still sit in this old inn yard just as they did four hundred years ago.

Mayors

The mayor was the most important citizen of the town in Tudor times. He was chosen by the people who owned property in the town.

Mayors who are elected today wear special robes and a chain with a badge. These are like the uniform of Tudor mayors.

Swearing in the mayor, Bristol 'Mayor's Kalendar', 1478

Mace, York

A large object called a mace has been carried in front of the mayor since Tudor times. This shows that he is important.

The mace was kept in the mayor's office. Today we call the mayor's office the City Hall, Town Hall or Guildhall.

 Town Hall clues:

Find out if your town has a mayor. How old is the town mace?

20

Aldeburgh, Suffolk

This Town Hall was built in 1540. In those days it had a thatched roof. Today it is still used for meetings of the Town Council.

One of the jobs that had to be done by a Tudor mayor was to make sure that the market was run fairly. Many towns had a proper set of weights and measures made. This was used to check that traders did not cheat their customers.

These weights were made in Queen Elizabeth's reign and kept by the Lord Mayor of London in the Guildhall.

 Street name clues about buying and selling:

Buttermarket, Peas Hill, Baker Street, Poultry, Cornhill.

Documents

Today, important documents are kept in the County Record Office, but in the past they were often kept in a special wooden box in the church.

> **Parish**
> A village and its people who are looked after by the vicar of the church.

One law passed in Tudor times said that the priest had to write down when anyone was born, got married or died. This was called keeping the **parish** 'register', the same word used for the book teachers have to keep today.

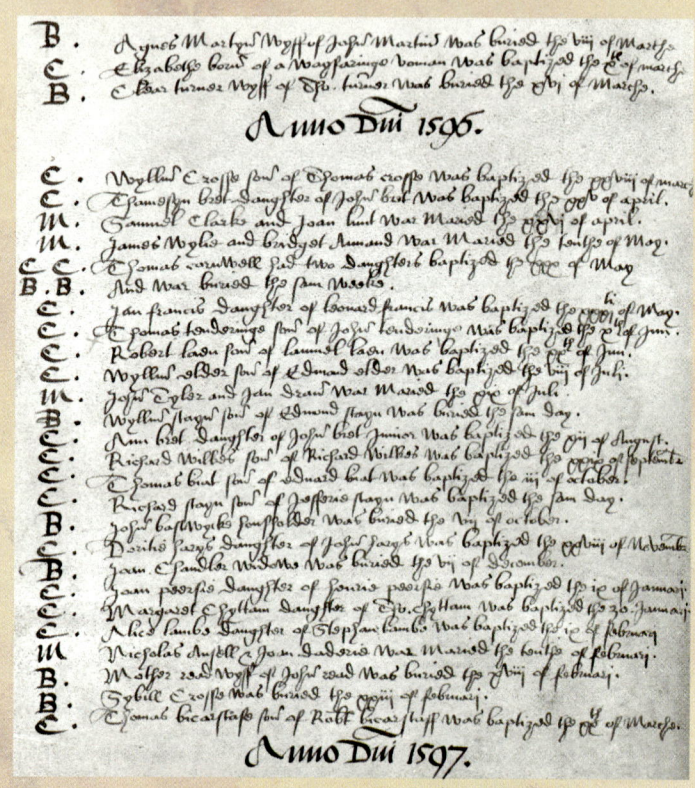

Parish record, Essex

The Tudors wrote with a **quill pen**. Their handwriting was different from ours.

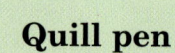

> **Quill pen**
> A pen made from a large feather, often a goose feather, sharpened at the end.

Not everyone could write in Tudor times. Some people asked the priest to write down what they wanted to do with the things they owned when they died.

John Underwood was a joiner who made things out of wood. He died on May 30, 1580. This is what he asked the priest to write down for him:

Apparel
Clothes

To Elizabeth my wife all my implements of household as brass, pewter, bedding and apparel, praying her to be good to my brother Robert Underwood in giving him houseroom and ministering to his necessity as occasion and her ability shall give.

More document clues:

Lists of things people owned when they died. These are called inventories.

Objects

Many objects used in Tudor times are now kept in museums. They help us to learn a lot about the people who lived then.

This pillow was made in Tudor times and filled with sweet-smelling herbs. We do not know who made it, but it still tells us some useful information about Tudor life:

- It is made from linen. Linen was made from a plant called flax that grew in the fields.

- Daffodils, honeysuckle, sweet peas and pinks grew in Tudor gardens.

- There were snails, butterflies, worms and birds in Tudor gardens.

 Objects in museums to look for:

Coins, tableware, needlework, weights and measures, jewellery, clothing.
Look at the materials they are made from and how they were decorated.